Go, Critter, Go!

Crawl, Ladybug, Crawl!

Dana Meachen Rau

Marshall Cavendish
Benchmark
New York

Ladybugs have black spots.

Ladybugs have red spots.

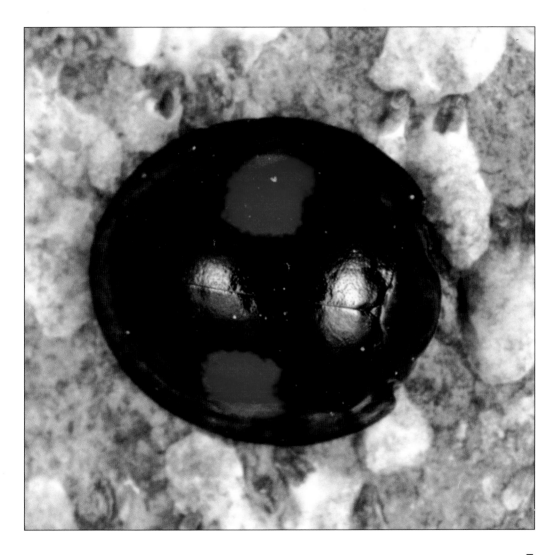

Ladybugs have two wings.

Ladybugs have six legs.

9

Ladybugs crawl on leaves.

Ladybugs eat bugs.

Ladybugs fly.

Ladybugs land.

Crawl, ladybug, crawl!

Words We Know

black spots

bugs

leaves

legs

red spots

wings

Index

About the Author

Dana Meachen Rau is an author, editor, and illustrator. A graduate of Trinity College in Hartford, Connecticut, she has written more than one hundred fifty books for children, including nonfiction, biographies, early readers, and historical fiction. She lives with her family in Burlington, Connecticut.

With thanks to the Reading Consultants:

Nanci Vargus, Ed.D., is an Assistant Professor of Elementary Education at the University of Indianapolis.

Beth Walker Gambro received her M.S. Ed. Reading from the University of St. Francis, Joliet, Illinois.

Marshall Cavendish Benchmark
99 White Plains Road
Tarrytown, New York 10591-9001
www.marshallcavendish.us

Library of Congress Cataloging-in-Publication Data

Rau, Dana Meachen, 1971–
Crawl, ladybug, crawl! / by Dana Meachen Rau.
p. cm. — (Bookworms. Go, critter, go!)
Summary: "Describes characteristics and behaviors of ladybugs"—Provided by publisher.
Includes index.
ISBN-13: 978-0-7614-2652-3
1. Ladybugs—Juvenile literature. I. Title. II. Series.
QL596.C65R38 2007
595.76'9—dc22
2006034229

Editor: Christina Gardeski
Publisher: Michelle Bisson
Designer: Virginia Pope
Art Director: Anahid Hamparian

Photo Research by Anne Burns Images

Cover Photo by *Peter Arnold Inc.*/PHONE/Jean-Michel Labat

The photographs in this book are used with permission and through the courtesy of:
Peter Arnold Inc.: pp. 1, 19 PHONE/Jean-Michel Labat; pp. 3, 20TL Jean-Jacques Etienne; pp. 7, 21B D. Bringard.
Corbis: pp. 5, 21TR Bob Marsh/Papilio; pp. 9, 21TL Ralph A. Clevenger; pp. 13, 20TR Anthony Bannister/Gallo Images.
Animals Animals: pp. 11, 20B Robert Maier; p. 15 Paulo De Oliveira; p. 17 Stephen Dalton.

Printed in Malaysia
3 5 6 4 2